Achieving Supervisory Excellence

Be the leader your people need

Rick Conlow
Doug Watsabaugh

Viva Books
New Delhi | Mumbai | Chennai | Kolkata
Bengaluru | Hyderabad | Kochi | Guwahati

First Indian Edition 2011

VIVA BOOKS PRIVATE LIMITED

- 4737/23 Ansari Road, Daryaganj, New Delhi 110 002
  E-mail: vivadelhi@vivagroupindia.net, Tel. 42242200
- 76, Service Industries, Shirvane, Sector 1, Nerul, Navi Mumbai 400 706
  E-mail: vivamumbai@vivagroupindia.net, Tel. 27721273, 27721274
- Jamals Fazal Chambers, 26 Greams Road, Chennai 600 006
  E-mail: vivachennai@vivagroupindia.net, Tel. 28290304, 28294241
- B-103, Jindal Towers, 21/1A/3 Darga Road, Kolkata 700 017
  E-mail: vivakolkata@vivagroupindia.net, Tel. 22836381, 22816713
- 7, Sovereign Park Apartments, 56-58, K. R. Road, Basavanagudi, Bengaluru 560 004
  E-mail: vivabangalore@vivagroupindia.net, Tel. 26607409, 26607410
- 101-102 Mughal Marc Aptt., 3-4-637 to 641, Narayanguda, Hyderabad 500 029
  E-mail: vivahyderabad@vivagroupindia.net, Tel. 27564481, 27564482
- First Floor, Beevi Towers, SRM Road, Kaloor, Kochi 682 018, Kerala
  E-mail: vivakochi@vivagroupindia.net, Tel: 0484-2403055, 2403056
- 232, GNB Road, Beside UCO Bank, Silpukhuri, Guwahati 781 003
  E-mail: vivaguwahati@vivagroupindia.net, Tel: 0361-2666386

www.vivagroupindia.com

Published by arrangement with

Axzo Press, LLC
562, Willow Brook Office Park
Fairport, New York 14450

ISBN : 978-81-309-1821-1

Published by Vinod Vasishtha for Viva Books Private Limited, 4737/23, Ansari Road, Daryaganj, New Delhi - 110 002. Printed and bound by Raj Press, R-3, Inderpuri, New Delhi - 110 012.

Table of Contents

About the Authors

Rick Conlow

Rick's clients have achieved double- and triple-digit improvement in their sales performance, quality, customer loyalty, and service results. These clients include organizations that are leaders in their industries, as well as others that are less recognizable. Regardless, their goals are his goals.

Rick's life view and extensive background in sales and leadership—as a general manager, vice president, training director, program director, national sales trainer, and consultant—are the foundation of his coaching, training, and consulting services. Participants in Rick's "live action" programs walk away with inspiration and skills they can immediately put to use.

These programs include *BEST Selling!, Moments of Magic!, Excellence in Management!, SuperSTAR Service and Selling!, The Greatest Secrets of all Time!*, and *Good Boss/Bad Boss: Which One Are You?* Rick has also written *Excellence in Management*, *Excellence in Supervision*, *Returning to Learning*, and *Moments of Magic*.

When he's not engaging an audience or engrossed in a coaching discussion, this proud husband and father is most likely astride a weight bench or riding a motorcycle, taking on the back roads and highways of Minnesota.

Doug Watsabaugh

Before starting his own business, Doug served as the director of operations for a national training institute, served as manager of organization development for a major chemical company, and was responsible for worldwide training and organization development for the world's third largest toy company. He was also a partner in Performance & Human Development LLC, a California company that published high-involvement experiential activities, surveys, instruments, interactive training modules, papers, and multimedia presentations.

Doug has co-authored two books with John E. Jones, Ph.D., and William L. Bearley, Ed. D.: *The New Fieldbook for Trainers,* published by HRD Press and Lakewood Publishing, and *The OUS Quality Item Pool*, about organizational survey items that measure Baldrige criteria.

He is a member of the American Society for Training and Development (ASTD), the Minnesota Quality Council, and The National Organization Development Network.

Preface

In a world of economic crisis and political instability, supervisory excellence is in great demand, and it is in short supply. Management gurus abound in giving advice. There are all sorts of theories from which to pick. What's a supervisor to do to be more effective? How can a supervisor significantly increase the productivity, customer service, quality, or other results of his or her employees? The bad news is that there isn't any magical formula for supervisory excellence.

The good news in *Achieving Supervisory Excellence* is that the things that bring success are achievable. Management consultant Peter Drucker said, "Don't worry about doing everything right, just do the right things." But what are the right things?

This book is not theory but an action-oriented book. The material evolved from over 25 years of experience in management and sales in the public and private sectors. Over that time, we have worked with and trained thousands of supervisors, managers, and executives. In the last ten years, keys to excellence have emerged that we put into a series of seminars called "Excellence in Supervision," "Excellence in Management," and "Excellence in Leadership." We have worked with, observed, and identified the approaches of the best leaders across multiple companies.

Whether you are a new manager (see our book *Becoming a Successful Supervisor*) or an experienced one, you can use *Achieving Supervisory Excellence* as a tool to keep yourself focused on the skills and techniques that will help you make a significant difference relatively quickly. As you work with the material, you will be required to make a personal commitment to change and grow. Mediocrity is unacceptable in the marketplace today. Why should it be acceptable for you? Even being good isn't good enough anymore. Business is too competitive and the challenges are too great to be content with the status quo. *Achieving Supervisory Excellence* includes the right things to empower you to become one of the best in your chosen field. Let's get started.

The behavior and characteristics of the best supervisors are evident from research and practical experience. Employees also know a poor or excellent supervisor when they see one, and by their experiences with one. Supervisors become poor or excellent managers by what they do or don't do. It's also about who you are as a person. The best supervisors have a sense of integrity that guides them to do the right things and to do them in the right way. However, excellent supervisors are made, not born. You can learn to do what the best supervisors do. You have to become a student of the game of leadership and supervision. This book will help you do that.

The objectives of this book deal with five strategies you can start using today to immediately begin making a difference in your job with the employees you work with.

Learning Objectives

Complete this book, and you'll know how to:

1) Establish high-performance goals and plans
2) Persuade others in a positive manner
3) Solve problems proactively
4) Supervise with flexibility
5) Lead a high-performance work environment

Workplace and Management Competencies mapping

For over 30 years, business and industry has utilized competency models to select employees. The trend to use competency-based approaches in education and training, assessment, and development of workers has experienced a more recent emergence within the Employment and Training Administration (ETA), a division of the United States Department of Labor.

The ETA's General Competency Model Framework spans a wide array of competencies from the more basic competencies, such as reading and writing, to more advanced occupation-specific competencies. The Crisp Series finds its home in what the ETA refers to as the Workplace Competencies and the Management Competencies.

Achieving Supervisory Excellence covers information vital to mastering the following competencies:

Workplace Competencies:

- Teamwork

Management Competencies:

- Supporting Others
- Motivating & Inspiring

About the Viva-Crisp 50-Minute Series

The Viva-Crisp 50-Minute Series was designed to cover critical business and professional development topics in the shortest possible time. Our easy-to-read, easy-to-understand format can be used for self-study or for classroom training. With a wealth of hands-on exercises, the 50-Minute books keep you engaged and help you retain critical skills.

What You Need to Know

We designed the Viva-Crisp 50-Minute Series to be as self-explanatory as possible. But there are a few things you should know before you begin the book.

Exercises

Exercises look like this:

EXERCISE TITLE

Questions and other information would be here.

Keep a pencil handy. Any time you see an exercise, you should try to complete it. If the exercise has specific answers, an answer key will be provided in the appendix. (Some exercises ask you to think about your own opinions or situation; these types of exercises will not have answer keys.)

Forms

A heading like this means that the rest of the page is a form:

FORMHEAD

Forms are meant to be reusable. You might want to make a photocopy of a form before you fill it out, so that you can use it again later.

A Note to Instructors

We've tried to make the Viva-Crisp 50-Minute Series books as useful as possible as classroom training manuals. Here are some of the features we provide for instructors:

- PowerPoint presentations
- Answer keys
- Assessments
- Customization

PowerPoint Presentations

You can download a PowerPoint presentation for this book from our Web site at www.CrispSeries.com.

Answer keys

If an exercise has specific answers, an answer key will be provided in the appendix. (Some exercises ask you to think about your own opinions or situation; these types of exercises will not have answer keys.)

Assessments

For each 50-Minute Series book, we have developed a 35- to 50-item assessment. The assessment for this book is available at www.CrispSeries.com. *Assessments should not be used in any employee-selection process.*

PART 1

Establish High-Performance Goals

> ***"The future always has depended on our ability to see new possibilities."***
>
> **–Unknown**

In this part:

- The High-Performance Formula
- Team Goals and Planning
- Employee Goals and Planning

The High-Performance Formula

The Drake Equation is as follows: N=RxFpNeFeFiFcL. It predicts how many planets are like earth in the known universe. There are other formulas in science, like $e=mc^2$ or $A=1/2B\times H$. You can count on their authenticity.

Here's a simple management formula for creating a high-performance environment, where employees want to do a good job and routinely go the extra mile. You can count on it.

> HP = CE(C+M+E)
>
> High Performance = Clear Expectations ×
> (Competence + Motivation + Environment)

Of course, this is a conceptual formula. That is, you won't actually plug numbers into it and get an answer. Rather, the formula reminds you of the crucial factors that contribute to supervising success.

High Performance

High performance means exceeding company goals and raising the standards for results. It also means finding ways to become consistently better. Eventually, it creates new potential boundaries and redefines what is really possible. Excellent supervisors inspire people to achieve high performance and to sustain it. They also create a climate where employees want to excel. Good supervision requires paying attention to their competence, their motivation, and the environment of the workplace.

Clear Expectations

Planning begins with establishing goals. You need to get these clarified to build a foundation of positive results. It is important both for you to know what is expected of you and for your employees to know what is expected of them.

Competence

Competence refers to the employee's job-related skills and knowledge. In any profession, the best performers continually practice and train to get better. A concert pianist puts in countless hours to play with effortless grace. Professional baseball players prepare in the winter and during spring training for the regular season and continue to practice before games throughout the year.

To compete today, supervisors need to educate and train their employees. We agree that companies should hire competent people first, but then you need to keep them learning. This is especially important if you can't always attract or afford the best talent. "World-class" training is usually equal to about 5% of your payroll budget. You might not have that kind of budget or a training department, but you don't really need it. Practically speaking; if you do on-the-job training and cross-train people for different jobs, and you do monthly training on procedures, safety, communication, customer service, quality, or product information, you will increase the skill and knowledge of your team. It's not always about teaching people new things—it's also about fine-tuning their current skills. In *Fortune* magazine's lists of the best companies to work for, the top 10 companies consistently provide an average of 50–60 hours of training per employee per year.

Motivation

Motivation is the employee's willingness and desire to do the job. Most people have this to a certain degree because they at least want a paycheck. Although they might like the job, they aren't doing it for free. The work and the income create the motivation to do the job.

But that's not enough today. Business is tough and competitive. We need stellar performances. How do you get people to go the extra mile routinely? Supervisors need highly productive people. How do you get them to come to work because they enjoy it? How do you get them to want to do the job better and better? What motivates people, really? Here's a thought: Which employee will perform better—the one you consistently build up or the one you verbally beat up?

Poor supervisors have a distorted view of their role in employee motivation. As you know, the airline industry has faced challenging times. Many blame it on high gas prices and 9/11. Southwest Airlines has prospered despite this tough environment. Why? They have cultivated better relationships with employees and customers than their competitors have. Southwest employees want to come to work, and they are the most productive in the industry. Southwest hires carefully, trains for excellence, gives plenty of recognition, and creates a fun, dynamic workplace. Southwest employees are among the leaders in productivity in the airline industry.

The other airlines have poorer relationships with employees and customers. One large airline has this unspoken philosophy for employees: *leave your brains at the door!* Not surprisingly, this airline has been in bankruptcy, and management continually has contentious relationships with employees and the unions. Less effective supervisors destroy employee commitment and the desire to excel. Their employees come to work for the paycheck. They just go through the motions on the job and they can't wait to go home. Many start looking for a better job. Unfortunately, some supervisors are oblivious to this employee condition.

Complete the exercise on the Ten Signs of Poor Supervisory Practices.

Ten Signs of Poor Supervisory Practices

Check the conditions you have seen in companies. Add two more from your own experience. Make a commitment to do better than this.

____ 1. High turnover

____ 2. Poor quality or customer service

____ 3. Poor productivity

____ 4. Above-average absenteeism rates

____ 5. Above-average sick days

____ 6. More grievances

____ 7. Excessive employee conflict

____ 8. More worker's compensation issues

____ 9. Inconsistent results

____ 10. Few new ideas from employees

____ 11. Other: ______________________________

____ 12. Other: ______________________________

Environment

This issue is all about the work environment. Is it supportive or not? Excellent supervisors are supportive; others aren't. A supportive environment involves:

- A positive atmosphere, not a negative one
- Clear goals, not vague directions
- Listening, not telling or yelling
- Recognition and praise, not constant criticism
- Communication, not conflict
- Social activities, not isolation
- Innovation, not the same old thing
- Continuous improvement, not "my way or the highway"
- Integrity, not disreputable practices
- Fun and challenging work, not boring and routine work

All good performance begins with clear goals and plans, for both you and your employees. All supervisors need to be crystal clear on three things to succeed:

1. What are the critical success factors—key goals—in my job? And what does a good job look like?
2. What resources—people, equipment, money—do I have to get the job done?
3. What's my plan to succeed? How will I do this well in the short term and get even better in the long term?

You start by focusing on your team goals and then drill down to individual employees and their responsibilities and expectations.

Team Goals and Planning

First of all, you need a planning process that is straightforward and specific. Most supervisors today are working in companies that are "lean and mean." This means that they have just enough people to get the job done. Most supervisors are not just the leader of their work teams, but are also required to do part of work. So they are working supervisors. Time is of the essence. Is that true for you?

Clarify the Expectations Your Company Has of You

Planning begins with establishing goals. You need to get these clarified to build a foundation of positive results. This means that you need to review your experience and how it relates to your role as supervisor. It also means having a conversation with your boss about your job responsibilities and how success will be measured. If you have done this before, great, but remember that it's an ongoing process.

One company set a goal of $300 a week in additional sales for each customer service representative. When the supervisors came together to plan how to do this, everyone had a different definition of what this meant. It took them half a day to pinpoint what the goal really was, and what management expected, so that everyone was on the same page. They then created a detailed action planning process to help them achieve the goal. By year's end, they had exceeded the goal by improving 122% over the previous year. Without this planning effort, they would never have accomplished this outstanding productivity.

You need to know the critical success factors for your job. Try the following exercise. What are the common elements in each area? They should be similar. If they aren't, review with your boss your understanding of his or her expectations.

"Well, I would have exhibited more leadership qualities if someone would have told me to."

CRITICAL SUCCESS FACTORS

In the spaces below, identify what is most crucial to your success from three perspectives: your experience, your job description, and your boss's communication.

Your experience: ____

____

____

____

Your job description: ____

____

____

____

Your boss's comments: ____

____

____

____

Set Three to Five SMART Goals

SMART goals are based on your critical success factors and are defined in the following manner:

- **Specific** — Is it focused?
- **Measurable** — Can you tell whether it has been accomplished?
- **Attainable** — Is it a realistic target?
- **Relevant** — Is it a priority?
- **Time-bound** — What is the timeline for review?

Through a couple of conversations, you should be able determine precisely what you are expected to do and then set goals and action steps. You take the time to do this to eliminate misunderstandings and the chance of failure.

The Best Supervisors Create Monthly Goals and Plans

A retail services company has over 400 locations in the U.S. By establishing goals and action plans for a new marketing campaign, the company achieved 57%–74% sales improvements, depending on the city, in just a few months. We observed that the leading supervisors had goals and plans, which they implemented on a monthly basis. A few times a month, they reviewed their progress. Every day throughout the month, they used spreadsheets, goal boards, surveys, tracking sheets, or other tools to consistently monitor their team's performance.

DRAFTING GOALS

Write a draft of your goals below.

Example 1: Achieve a customer satisfaction rating of 95% each month.

Example 2: Achieve 2% or less accounts at 90 days Accounts/Receivable (A/R) every month.

Identifying Action Plans

The complexity of your job will determine how detailed your action plans are. If you are supervising production lines in an assembly plant with robotics, you might have separate action plans for every goal. If you are a supervisor at a fast-food restaurant, you might have one action plan for your goals. Be as specific as you need to be to reach your goals.

Also, engage your employees in your planning process. Again, the more complex the job, the higher the required education level; and the more professional the job, the more you want to involve employees. Engagement and involvement build commitment to the plan, provide you with better ideas, strengthen teamwork, and heighten employee motivation. They also give everyone a growth opportunity in problem solving and help you assess the team skills of your people. Supervisors don't have all the answers, and most people want to be included so they can contribute to progress in a meaningful way.

Most plans can be created in a few meetings of 30–60 minutes each. Document your efforts and establish a mechanism for tracking results and holding people accountable for doing their part.

CREATING ACTION PLANS

Write a draft of your plans below.

Example 1: Monitor customer surveys daily. Call everyone who responded, whether their responses were positive or negative. Thank the people with positive responses and see if there is anything else we can do for them. Fix the problems of those with negative responses. (All line supervisors will do this. This will amount to about 15–20 calls a week.)

Example 2: Keep a weekly tracking board for all in the department to see our results over time as it relates to the goal. (Joe will do this.)

TEAM GOAL SETTING AND PLANNING

In spaces below, finalize your goals and plans for your department. Review the goals with your team and boss. Then act with consistency and passion.

Team goals:

Team action steps:

Employee Goals and Planning

Goal setting really works, yet few supervisors do it well. If they set goals at all, it often only involves saying, "I want you here every day at work and we'll get along fine!" Showing up for work or being on time is no big deal. Employees need more than that. Employees need goals and a challenge. It helps them perform better. Can you imagine a distance runner running a race not knowing the distance or being timed? Can you imagine playing football or soccer without goal lines or keeping track of the score?

Ask your employees what their goals are. Most won't know or will utter general remarks like:

- To take care of the customer
- To make a living
- To do a good job
- To keep a job
- To make my boss happy
- To survive
- To get the job done

If your employees make comments like these, they might be sincere and they might be trying, or they might not care, but they are not doing their best. It's a supervisor's responsibility to help employees get beyond this barrier to excellence.

Setting Goals

It's hard work being a supervisor with employees who lack goals and who show up for work each day just for a paycheck. It's easier and more fun being a supervisor with employees who have goals, are excited about what they are doing, and come to work because they enjoy the challenges of the job. Why? Employees with goals improve their performance. A book entitled *Goal Setting: A Motivational Technique That Works*, by Edwin Locke and Gary Latham, identifies research studies that found that in 90% of the cases, goal setting increased employees' performance. Locke and Latham looked at jobs in several areas, including data entry, production, customer service, and sales. They concluded that goal setting will, if properly done, motivate employees to increase their efforts. It is the one management technique that consistently works because it establishes expectations and provides a way to give feedback on results. Most people deep down what to win, to do a good job, and to have pride in their work.

Setting Employee SMART Goals

How do you set goals with employees? There are two ways:

- Set goals *for* the employee.
- Set goals *with* the employee.

Either way works, but the second way tends to be more effective. The reason is that the employee is more committed if she has participated in making the goal. She has ownership of the goal and the outcome. When you set goals, set SMART goals, as we have discussed. Here are a few examples:

- Like this: To sell $15,000 in parts the first quarter.

  Not like this: To sell more.

- Like this: To handle all customer complaints within 48 hours, using the ACT form for documentation.

  Not like this: To satisfy customers.

- Like this: To answer the phone within 3 rings and say: "Good morning, Rosebud Company. This is Mary. How may I help you?"

  Not like this: Do a better job on the phone.

Set goals and develop plans with employees at the times listed below:

1. During the interview. (Review job expectations and goals.)
2. First day on the job.
3. First week on the job.
4. First month on the job.
5. First 90 days on the job.
6. Quarterly. (Review goals with employees one on one. This is a minimum expectation. Monthly is better. This is informal and we will discuss this more shortly.)
7. Yearly or every six months, depending on your company's guidelines for performance reviews. (This review is more in-depth than the other ones and involves a discussion on compensation. Talk to your human resources or personnel department about how your company handles this.

This process does take time and is hard work. Why so much? Eighty percent of job performance problems are the result of a lack of clear expectations and goals and the lack of recognition. Most supervisors and managers don't handle this situation well, so it becomes a differentiator for achieving excellence. Invest the time, learn to master the process, and you will save time later and have a high-performance team.

When you do this goal-setting process, start with one of your experienced employees and ask her to fill out the High-Performance Planning Form. Tell her it's a way for you to better support her and to help her succeed on the job. Explain that you will talk to her about it in a couple of days.

Next, you fill out the page yourself, and when you meet with the employee, discuss the information. Talk to the employee about goals on a regular basis. Eventually, do this with all your employees.

Keep this process informal by using the form in the following activity or just using a sheet of paper. Keep the completed forms on file for review and documentation. Keep in mind that this is not a performance planning and review effort. This is a communication, expectation, and motivation process designed to accomplish the following objectives:

- Create an avenue for the supervisor and employee to discuss the employee's job duties and performance on a regular basis, and to do this without money issues or salary increases creating unnecessary pressures.
- Head off problems early and give the supervisor an easy opportunity to give feedback, recognition, and constructive guidance for improvement.
- Focus on goals, not on problems.
- Give employees a forum for input about their jobs. This builds commitment and motivation for a more successful effort.

Employee Reponses to Goal Setting and Planning

If you take this goal setting approach, as the best supervisors and managers do, how do you think your employees will respond? Responses often include ones like these:

- **Wait and see** — Does the manager really mean it?
- **Resentment** — I'm an experienced employee; I don't need this.
- **Excitement** — I'll turn my High-Performance Goal Form into a 10-page term paper
- **Acceptance** — Especially from new employees.

Regardless of how your employees respond, you must follow through. One supervisor started the process and it didn't work. He told the employees to get back to him when they finished filling out the form. Guess what? The employees didn't get back to him! So you have to do the follow-up, or your effort is wasted!

If the employee doesn't fill out his or her form, give the person time to do it at your first meeting. Then discuss it. Explain the concept, get it started, and then do the follow-up meeting, in which you and the employee discuss the key points. If you follow through and do the process for your department and each team member time and again, it works!

HIGH-PERFORMANCE PLANNING FORM

Name: ______________________________

Priorities: ______________________________

____

____

Strengths: ______________________________

____

____

Areas to improve: ______________________________

____

____

Goals: ______________________________

____

____

Action steps: ______________________________

____

____

____

____

One supervisor held a meeting with his employees to set goals and create plans to accomplish a major project. The project had a short timeline and had to be completed for the customer on time. All other work had to be done as well. In addition, the supervisor had no funds for incentives or bonuses. Through open communication, the group agreed to a productivity goal; the reward was a day off with pay later. Results were tracked on charts for all to see. The employees achieved the goal by increasing productivity 25%!

CASE STUDY: An Excellent Supervisor

Shirley is a production supervisor in a large metropolitan business. She has 40 direct reports. The employees, called associates, perform a variety of jobs. After attending an Excellence in Management seminar, Shirley started setting goals and plans with her associates. The goal related to monthly productivity.

Shirley divided her employees into seven teams. She held a meeting with each team to begin the process. Each team created a name for itself and made charts to track progress. They agreed that if they hit the goal, Shirley would buy lunch. One action step the team came up with called for more cross-training.

In the first six months of the process, teams' productivity soared and reached or exceeded the goal five times. Each time, Shirley bought lunch to reward the effort. Shirley and her associates have maintained their success.

What are the strategies Shirley used?

____

____

____

What can you learn or relearn from this?

____

____

____

____

Compare your answers to the authors' suggested responses in the Appendix.

Part Summary

In this part, you learned about what motivates and inspires employees. You and your employees will be able to set reachable goals and become more motivated. Not only will you be more satisfied with your work, but you will also create a positive work environment for your employees.

PART 2

Persuade Positively

"Leaders must communicate the vision in a way that attracts and excites members of the organization."

–David Berlew

In this part:

- Influence Positively
- Build Trust and Rapport
- Listen Effectively

Influence Positively

The High-Performance Formula gives us a roadmap to motivating people. It begins with establishing clear goals and expectations. Establishing the goals, though, is only the beginning. In the daily application of the work, we need to communicate with, influence, and persuade people to accomplish the job well. We need to do this every day with people, one on one and as a team. You need trust and rapport with people to most effectively motivate them. Building this kind of relationship takes some hard work. Trust and rapport don't just come with the title; they must be earned.

What Motivates People?

In his article "One more time: How do you motivate employees?" Frederick Herzberg seems irritated by leaders' continued problems with motivation. According to Herzberg, the factors that motivate most people are achievement, recognition, the work itself, responsibility, advancement, growth, and learning. Our opportunity as supervisors is to leverage these factors to enrich employees' jobs.

Notice that money isn't on the list. Herzberg argues that a monetary incentive is more of a "kick in the pants" than a motivator. A kick in the pants can be negative or positive, fear-based or monetary-incentive-based. Herzberg says both approaches produce movement, but not motivation. Movement means that there is a change in results, but largely because the supervisor took action rather than the employee. Motivation that means the employee has an impetuous to do the job better or more effectively and isn't influenced by an external reward.

Studies of total quality management find that employees are most motivated or satisfied by:

- Interesting and challenging work
- Recognition
- The feeling of being "in on" things
- Benefits
- Pay

What do you think was at the top of the supervisors' list? Their top five were money, benefits, working conditions, recognition, and challenging work. Why the difference? All too often, supervisors don't understand motivation and don't give employees what they want or need in a job.

Motivating people is seldom easy. So how do you motivate people? You don't! In fact, many experts say you don't motivate others; you can only create positive conditions so people motivate themselves.

Your efforts will be more effective if you take into account three important factors. Each condition must be fulfilled—and built upon—before you can move on to the next one.

1. First, all people want something. It might be more money, a promotion, job satisfaction—anything. They must desire it strongly enough to be willing to do something to get it. As a supervisor, you need to know what it is and turn it into a tangible goal. If people have no goals or desires, you'll get no motivation from them. Unmotivated employees show little initiative or progress. However, everyone has some motivation. A successful supervisor will find the "hot button."

2. Second, people need to know what steps to take to succeed. It does no good to want something when there is no practical, visible way of ever achieving it. When people have a method or a plan for success, they get motivated. If they are given the tools and support to succeed, they will succeed. An essential step in motivating anyone is to identify or create the path that must be traveled. Then, a supervisor needs to help by removing barriers and smoothing out the bumps.

3. Third, people must believe that their efforts will be meaningful and rewarded. Many people have goals, know what to do to achieve them, but lack the belief that their efforts will be recognized or have value. Recognition is the payoff; it makes the goals and effort worthwhile. Although recognition means different things to different people, it adds fuel to the flame of desire so that motivation continues in spite of obstacles.

If you want your people to achieve high performance, then you have to achieve it first. This begins with your Mental Models.

Mental Models

All of us have a way we look at the world. It's based on our experiences, background, education, religion, family, moods, fears, goals, successes, and failures. We call it our Mental Model. It affects our perception of the world and how we relate to others. What do you see in each of these pictures?

In the first slide, did you see the face and the word liar? In the second, slide did you see three faces: a young woman, an old woman, and a man with a moustache? And in the third slide, did you see the woman's face and the man playing a saxophone? Chances are, you saw some of these and missed others. These slides illustrate what happens to us in life. Our Mental Models filter out what disagrees with how we see things and lets in only what reinforces our way of thinking. As leaders of others, we become more effective if we can expand our view of the world to better understand the subtlety of situations and people.

Build Trust and Rapport

Building trust and rapport is about getting along with other people. It's not something that people seem to work at, yet most people believe they are good at it.

A speaker at a convention asked his audience members to stand if they couldn't get along with other people. No one stood up. Finally, after some silence a young man stood up in the back of the room. The speaker asked, "Young man, you mean to tell me that you can't get along with other people?" The man replied, "Oh sure I can. But I felt sorry for you standing up there all by yourself."

The Road to Good Rapport

People don't get along because they don't work at it or don't know how. It's often because they are too selfish, looking out for number one. Remember the bumper sticker, "He who dies with the most toys wins." So what's the answer for a supervisor who wants to motivate or influence others positively? Here are five concepts that help.

1. **Genuine concern** — This is where the process begins.
2. **Common ground** — Emphasize your similarities, not differences.
3. **Body language** — Put people at ease and be consistent.
4. **Tone of voice** — Be expressive, and pay attention to your impact on others.
5. **Mood** — Control your emotions and empathize with others.

Genuine Concern

Successful communication starts with an attitude. Author and motivator Zig Ziglar declares, "Give other people what they want and you'll get what you want." Notice how he said this. First you give, then you get. It isn't the other way around. This attitude is based on the Golden Rule. And yes, it is a concept that applies in any organization. Tom Peters, who co-wrote the book *In Search of Excellence* with Bob Waterman, says that they tried to identify policies, structures, and procedures that made a company great. Instead, they found intangibles—enthusiasm, pride, respect, caring, fun, and love. If you want to communicate effectively with people, you have to change your approach by giving more. First, ask yourself, how can I help others? Do this before you ask them to help you.

Common Ground

A very successful salesperson once explained his success this way: "I find common ground or interest with everyone. If people like fishing, we talk about it. If they are into sports, so am I. If they are older, I become the long-lost son. I'm like a chameleon."

A key to influencing others is establishing connections through common ground or interest. Do you know the things that interest your employees? Learn more about your employee's background, experiences, and family. The same is true for that difficult person to talk to. You can do this easily through small talk and revealing some things about yourself. Do this a little at a time, and you will learn a great deal about the people you work with. The goal here is to emphasize your similarities and not your differences. This all helps create empathy as well as understanding.

Body Language

A study indicated three major areas that affect the results of communication the most:

- Words
- Voice tone
- Body language

What percentages fall in each area? Words account for 7% of your communication impact. Voice tone equals 38%. Body language influences the outcome 55%. Isn't that amazing? What you say is one thing. How you say it is more significant. What you do about what you say is most powerful.

To match someone's body language, sit as he sits. Cross your arms if he does. Mirror the gestures and shifts in position. Never mimic; do everything subtly! It'll make an impact that says, "You can trust me; I'm like you."

Then, make an effort to use open and inviting body movements. Leaning forward, nodding yes, making eye contact, taking notes, and paraphrasing for understanding are examples. Watch out for the defensive approaches like eye rolling, frowning, folded arms, and leaning away.

Tone of Voice

The skill of using your voice well is helpful, too. Observe and listen to the person you talk to. Does she speak fast or slowly? Does she speak in short sentences or long ones? Does she have a low voice or a high one? Adjust your speech and tone to be similar. We once lost a client because he was slow and methodical in his discussion. We were more concerned about our product and gave a loud, over-exuberant presentation. We scared him and he didn't talk to us again. It was our mistake for not understanding what was comfortable for him as the customer.

Mood

Acknowledging and even matching a person's mood can be helpful. This is especially critical with an angry person. Become angry yourself. Don't be angry at the person—just match the intensity of the mood. Show immediate concern and a desire to take action. Acknowledge that the person has a right to be upset and that you'll get on it. There is a proverb that says, "He who is cheerful in the morning is counted as a curse." In other words, if two people's moods don't match, chances are they won't communicate well.

How Does This Relate to Achieving Supervisory Excellence?

These five concepts are ways to build individual credibility, establish teamwork, and win over difficult or different people. Each approach has to be naturally applied in daily situations over time to be effective. However, each concept can rapidly improve results and relationships. Try the next exercise.

Communication Climates

To become an excellent supervisor, you need to learn to communicate more effectively. How well you do this will make or break your success. You have to be willing to do what others never do or do only some of the time. Remember these words of motivator Zig Ziglar: "The greatest enemy of excellence is good."

Whenever two people meet, a communication climate forms between them. Sometimes it's positive and sometimes it's negative.

The communication climate can be like the weather; there are distinct signs that give you clues to what's happening. For example, imagine a cloudless day, about 80 degrees with a 5- to 10-mph breeze. Now imagine a day with high humidity and the temperature falling rapidly from the high 90s to the low 80s. It's dark, and there are fast-spinning clouds filling the sky. Do you know what is happening?

The communication climate affects how people communicate. It has more to do with behavior than with attitude. It can be positive or negative. The good news is that because it is caused by what people do, it can be managed.

For example, let's say you're talking to an employee about a personal problem. You never make eye contact and you talk to her while reading a report. What do you think the employee will feel? Or let's say you're talking to a customer. You welcome him cordially, offer him a cup of coffee, sit at a round table, make appropriate eye contact, and discuss his needs. Do you think the results will be more favorable than in the earlier example? Absolutely.

Your Communication Climate

Consciously or subconsciously, you do things that contribute to the communication climate you create with any individual. Here are five keys:

1. What you do is of utmost importance. You can't control what the other person does. You can control what you do.
2. Some of your behaviors are positive.
3. Some of your behaviors are negative.
4. In each case, you don't always know what you do that makes a difference.
5. By becoming more aware of what contributes to a positive or a negative climate, you can make changes to be more effective.

COMMUNICATION CLIMATE CHECKLIST

Read the lists below, and think about how each item can affect communication. Then think about some recent conversations you've had. Circle five items in the positive column that you think you need to do more, and circle three items in the negative column that you think you need to do less. How can you eliminate these negatives today? How can you use your strengths more effectively? Write your responses below.

Positive Communication	Negative Communication
1. Listened (restated problem)	1. Lacked eye contact
2. Had good eye contact	2. Acted hostile
3. Talked as an equal	3. Sat behind a desk
4. Gave full and prompt attention	4. Didn't ask any questions
5. Asked questions	5. Looked at watch
6. Smiled	6. Acted defensive
7. Used firm handshake	7. Didn't smile
8. Gave compliments	8. Slouched
9. Was courteous	9. Used monotone voice
10. Stood and sat straight	10. Showed no sincerity
11. Was enthusiastic	11. Didn't follow through
12. Stayed on subject	12. Used bad language
13. Used positive verbal cues	13. Was sarcastic
14. Eliminated barriers	14. Rushed the problem or person
15. Stayed positive	15. Criticized others
16. Other ____________	16. Other ____________
17. Other ____________	17. Other ____________

Listen Effectively

Successful salesman, businessman, and motivator Bob Conklin says, "To listen, you must want to listen." That's the first ingredient. Do you care enough to pay attention? All excellent supervisors are good listeners. They take time to hear the problems of subordinates, co-workers, or customers.

There are many barriers to effective listening. Here are some of them:

- Noise distractions
- Interruptions
- Differences of opinion
- Prejudices, biases
- Different priorities
- Busyness
- Lack of interest
- Limited time
- Thinking of other things
- Thinking someone is wrong
- Tiredness
- Perception differences

Listening can be tough work. Unfortunately, few supervisors or people in general know how to listen effectively. Often the only reason employees say they don't feel appreciated is that no one listens properly to their concerns.

How to Listen

As stated earlier, first you have to want to listen. There are other techniques that help as well. Each is described below:

- Making eye contact
- Limiting barriers
- Using the person's name
- Paraphrasing what's said
- Listening actively

Making Eye Contact

In our society, we don't lock eyeballs; that's intimidating. We use the glance-away method instead. Look at your partner for three or four seconds; then quickly look down or to the side. Then make eye contact again. Proper eye contact expresses interest and empathy. One consultant is so adroit at this that her co-workers and customers call it uncanny. Anyone who talks to her feels special and feels that they really matter.

Limiting Barriers

Ask the person to sit down if appropriate, and meet so you have privacy. Sit at a round table or to the side of your desk. Put the phone on hold, move away from the computer, and set that report off to the side. Lean forward and in toward the employee. Face the person directly. Don't fold your arms. Keep them on your lap or desk. Take notes if appropriate. (Tell the employee before you do). Put your feet flat on the floor. Use this approach in the beginning of the meeting to express your concern and willingness to be involved.

Using a Person's Name

Use it. By using a person's name, you demonstrate a positive relationship and interest. You'll also get the person's attention.

Paraphrasing

At an appropriate time in the conversation (or whenever you think you're receiving too much information to remember or understand), repeat to the person what she told you. Use your own words, of course. Start a paraphrase like this:

"If I understand you correctly…"

"What I hear you saying is…"

Don't say bland phrases like, "I understand." This isn't a paraphrase. Also, avoid saying, "What you really mean is _________." This is nothing more than an attempt to put words into someone's mouth or interpret someone's statement.

Listening Actively

By listening to someone, you are not necessarily agreeing with the person. The major goal of the listening technique is to better understand the employee. To be an active listener, you have to engage in the conversations:

- **Verbal cues** — "Uh-huh," "I see," "Yes," "Okay."
- **Nonverbal cues** — Nod your head on occasion, take notes, make eye contact.
- **Clarifying statements** — "Tell me more about that," "Give me an example."
- **Ask questions** — "What happened then?" "What else did you do?"

During your communication, it's your goal to express interest and concern in the employee's problems or ideas.

Three Ways to Apply Your Communication Skills

Create SMART goals to measure your progress in effective communication. You can significantly improve your results by applying your skills with employees through one-on-one sessions, regular department meetings, and to borrow a Tom Peters term, "Management By Wandering Around" (MBWA). Through the coaching process, you can discover how to apply your skills more effectively.

One-on-One Coaching Sessions

Supervisors can't lead merely through team meetings. While group meetings are important, a supervisor also needs to meet one-on-one with his or her employees. This means monthly to quarterly goal-setting sessions, and coaching sessions when appropriate. The goal of coaching is to develop an employee's skills to improve performance. It's a discovery and questioning process. A manager's job is to help the employee solve his or her own problems. Through a mutual decision-making process, discussion is held to improve results. Usually, this requires weekly meetings of about 30–60 minutes. Remember to focus on a goal, assess performance, give guidance, create a plan, and set follow-up steps.

Team Meetings

Regular team meetings are important for any supervisor or manager. Each meeting needs an agenda and a time limit. Most meetings can be completed in one-half to one and one-half hours. Remember to start on time and end on time. Too often, meetings lack agendas and timeframes, and countless hours are wasted because of pointless meetings, people coming late, lack of accountability, and extended timeframes. Be different; do it right. Here's why you have meetings:

- Share company news and results
- Celebrate success
- Discuss and create plans and goals
- Solve problems and brainstorm improvements
- Build teamwork and morale

Your agenda can generally follow this format for discussion: results, recognition, updates, plans or problems, new business, and next steps.

MBWA

Management consultant Tom Peters advocates Managing By Wandering Around. MBWA allows you to have informal and spontaneous conversations with employees and to refresh your own ideas with the changing scenery.

Jim was a super-successful general manager with over 40 years of practical experience. To what does he attribute his success? He always walked around the business before he went to his office. During his walks, he talked to people about things other than business. He got to know people and learned about their lives. If they wanted to talk business, they brought it up. While he didn't talk to everyone every day, he talked to different people each day. He learned to understand his people, their needs, and their issues. When problems arose, he received excellent input because of the trust and credibility that was established. This is MBWA!

LISTENING CHECKLIST

How do you rate on the Listening Quiz? Be honest and go to work on improving your listening skills. You'll become a better supervisor.

Fill out the listening quiz. Then have an employee or co-worker fill it out for you. What did you learn? Rate yourself on a scale of 1 to 5 for each item.

1 = Never, 2 = Rarely, 3 = Sometimes, 4 = Usually, 5 = Always

____ 1. Do you want to listen?

____ 2. Do you put what you are doing out of sight and out of mind?

____ 3. Do you make eye contact?

____ 4. Do you ignore or eliminate distractions?

____ 5. Do you smile, nod your head, and otherwise encourage the other person to talk?

____ 6. Do you think about what you will say?

____ 7. Do you try to figure out what the other person means through clarification?

____ 8. Do you try to figure out why the person is saying it?

CONTINUED

CONTINUED

____ 9. Do you let the other person finish what he or she is trying to say?

____ 10. If the person hesitates, do you encourage him or her to go on?

____ 11. Do you restate or paraphrase what the person says and ask if you got it right?

____ 12. Do you withhold judgment about the idea or problem until the person is finished talking?

____ 13. Do you listen regardless of the person's manner of speaking and choice of words?

____ 14. Do you listen even though you anticipate what the person is going to say?

____ 15. Do you question the person in order to get him or her to explain the idea more fully?

____ 16. Do you ask what is meant by some words to eliminate misunderstanding later?

How Well Do You Listen?

80–70	Excellent! You do a fine job of listening.
69–59	Your efforts are positive and done well.
58–48	Some areas are fine and above average. Pick a few areas to work on.
47 or less	Listening is a skill that can be learned. Practice to improve; it will make a difference in your communication with others.

Part Summary

From this part, you will be better able to develop communication skills that will help you connect positively with your employees. We've established the methods of creating an effective communication climate, influencing people in a positive manner, and building trust and rapport. You've also learned what you might need to work on in the areas of listening and creating common ground. You're on your way to making your employees more satisfied, which will, in turn, make your customers more satisfied.

PART 3

Solve Problems Proactively

> "*People don't leave for money,... they often leave for supervisors.*"
>
> **–Adrian Gostick and Chester Elton**

In this part:

- Performance Problems
- Conflict Problems

Performance Problems

Problems are inevitable. If you don't have problems, you're probably not taking risks as you strive to improve your efforts. The best supervisors work proactively to solve their employee performance problems and other work-related problems. We will work on two major areas of problems:

- Employee performance issues
- Work-related conflicts or problems

Employee Performance Issues

Here are three principles to handle common work-related problems:

- Handle it immediately.
- Be specific about the problem.
- Use one of three approaches to help:
  - Redirect
  - Review
  - Reprimand

Handle It Immediately

At this point, you're not trying to fire someone. Your goal is to get the employee to stay focused and do the job right. So handle the problem promptly. If an employee has a performance problem, confront it. Why wait? Don't save up a month's worth of issues and dump them on the employee all at once. The person will feel threatened and attacked. For example, if an employee's quality of work is declining, you need to identify that as soon as it's noticeable. Don't wait until it's a disaster.

On the other hand, don't nitpick everything that's wrong. Remember, if you make it a practice to give recognition and praise for a job well done, employees are more likely to hear your feedback on areas in which they don't do well.

Be Specific

Describe the behavior or action that is incorrect. "I saw you punching the button three times instead of two. That's why the part is below tolerance," or "In today's meeting, you criticized the team's efforts four times. You said…."

If you use generalities like "You are below performance" or "You have a bad attitude," your team won't know what you mean. You need to zero in. "On your last phone call, I heard you tell the customer, we are always behind schedule." Be specific and then review better ways of handling situations and your expectations.

Three Approaches That Help

How you handle a problem should also be situational. Here are three approaches that can help you motivate people as you deal with their performance issues.

Redirect. Communicate clearly about the job and how to do it. This is an on-the-job training process. Remember, this isn't a one-time thing. You will have to do this multiple times as a person learns a job, until he becomes proficient. Of course, different people learn at different speeds. Use redirection with new employees or employees inexperienced at a certain task.

- **Present** — Teach the employee how to do it by showing her first. Give directions in writing, too.
- **Practice** — Let the employee practice while you help.
- **Perform** — Give the employee time to work alone.
- **Evaluate** — Review progress, emphasize the positive, correct mistakes, and start over.

Review. Coach effectively! Work with the employee by asking questions to help the person learn through self-analysis. By getting involved in the process, the employee will be more committed.

- **Identify the goal or problem** — Work with inexperienced and experienced people. Make sure that goals are clarified and expectations understood. Ask, what are the goals? What is the issue? How have you tried to fix it? Be a good listener.
- **Discuss the problem** — Analyze what's happened so far. Ask, what's working? What hasn't worked? What have you learned? What do you think should be done differently?
- **Assess the level of performance** — Based on employee answers to your questions, begin identifying what needs to be done. Don't give advice yet.
- **Identify an action plan** — With the employee, create an action plan. Ask, what can you do to improve performance? Now provide advice, feedback, and specific expectations.
- **Follow up effectively** — Employee performance is often adversely affected by the lack of reinforcement by the leader. Once you have a plan, make sure you check back or have one-on-one sessions to review progress.

Reprimand. Use this approach if you have done the other steps and have seen no improvement. Confront the employee constructively. Do your homework so you know the situation. This is not a dialogue. Use this approach mainly with experienced employees. We don't use it with trainees or learners because they lack the experience to know how to do the job right. The exception is if the employee breaks a known policy or procedure.

- ▶ **Remember to be immediate and specific** — For a reprimand to be helpful, it needs to be timely and specific.
- ▶ **Share your feelings** — "I'm upset because you didn't get the report completed on time as we agreed." Employees need to experience the importance of this, and that's why you share your feelings. Don't yell, scream, or use foul language; it's unprofessional.
- ▶ **Explain what you want and the consequences** — "I want the report on Tuesday morning. If it's not ready, next time I'll give you a written warning."
- ▶ **Reaffirm the person** — Because the person is experienced, he or she can do the job and understand the expectation. Reaffirm the person's ability. "I know you can do this. You are one of my most reliable people." This will help the person focus on the problem, not on your leadership style.

When using the reprimand, be firm and focused. Again, don't yell, swear, or belittle the person. Focus on the behavior or issue; don't beat up the person. Most people want to do a good job, but like most of us, they sometimes they make mistakes. Be helpful, be firm, and take a caring approach while focusing on the need to get the job done.

Try the exercise on handling employee performance issues to pull all of these concepts together.

> ***"Fail to honor people, they fail to honor you. But of a good leader, who talks little, when his work is done, his aim fulfilled, they will all say, 'We did this ourselves.'"***
>
> **–Lao Tzu**

EMPLOYEE PERFORMANCE PROBLEMS

Check each problem that you've handled. Then circle three issues that you currently face. Remember the three key approaches: redirect, review, and reprimand.

____ 1. Poor performance or productivity

____ 2. Poor-quality work

____ 3. Abuse of company policy

____ 4. Theft

____ 5. Tardiness

____ 6. Absenteeism

____ 7. Dishonesty

____ 8. Customer complaints

____ 9. Discourtesy

____ 10. Insubordination

____ 11. Being critical of other employees

____ 12. Conflicts with other employees

____ 13. Poor appearance

____ 14. Lack of follow-through

____ 15. Poor communication with others

____ 16. Harassment

____ 17. Other (add a problem you face that is not listed) ______________

____

Performance Problems Checklist

Here's a separate checklist to remind you how to handle performance problems.

Redirect

- ❑ Present the problem
- ❑ Give the employee time to practice while you observe
- ❑ Encourage the employee to perform the task
- ❑ Evaluate results

Review

- ❑ Identify the goal or problem
- ❑ Discuss the problem: listen and ask questions
- ❑ Assess the level of performance
- ❑ Identify an action plan
- ❑ Follow up with next steps

Reprimand

- ❑ Be immediate and specific
- ❑ Share your feelings
- ❑ Explain what you want and the consequences of failure
- ❑ Reaffirm the employee

Conflict Problems

Conflict can be good. A manager without occasional conflicts within his team lacks real credibility. Conflicts arise from a variety of sources:

- Differences of opinion
- Team conflicts
- Technology or equipment problems
- Process improvements
- Human resources issues
- Interpersonal issues
- Customer complaints
- Quality or service concerns

Conflict is always present whether or not you recognize it, but conflict does not have to be negative. How you handle conflict greatly influences your team's cohesiveness and ability to work together effectively. Excellent supervisors deal with conflict constructively and create trust, credibility, and rapport with their teams. Poor supervisors avoid or dismiss conflict and consequently denigrate their integrity and that of the team.

Why is it important to deal with conflict? Primarily, because it is the honest thing to do. People don't always agree with each other; conflict is inevitable. But conflict doesn't require that people fight, yell, or scream at one another. If you want healthy and positive working relationships, conflict requires that you communicate and work through problems.

Conflict management is modeled by the team leader—by you, the boss. Your employees will mimic how you handle conflict. If you dismiss, avoid, or excessively delay dealing with conflict, your team members will likewise be hesitant to address issues. An unresolved conflict usually festers and gets worse, weakens communication, destroys trust, and results in ineffective performance.

By dealing with conflict quickly and effectively, you create an atmosphere that promotes positive communication and increases the quality and efficiency of your work. When issues are brought out in the open, they don't have a chance to stew. Opinions are heard, decisions are made, people feel better, and things get done.

How Does An Effective Supervisor Handle Conflict?

Start by letting your team members know that you value open communication. Let team members know you want to hear about their issues and problems, and that you want—and expect—them to offer solutions as well. Communicate this openness early and often in your work relationships.

Next, openly and constructively address the issues you observe. If an employee does something you don't like, approach the subject and state the issue without being judgmental. For example, say, "Bill, I noticed you changed the procedure we have for handling customer complaints. Tell me about your plan. I appreciate your reasons, but we will be unable to do that at this time because we can't support it with the current company resources. I expect you to immediately begin following the current procedure." An inquiry such as this gives Bill a chance to explain his motivation and intentions.

Similarly, if employees deliver bad news or report on a problem, remain objective and thank them for the information. Don't "kill the messenger" who brings negative information.

"We're going to stay in this room until we absolutely freakin' love each other."

Disagreements between employees require some careful handling. Here are some suggestions:

- If it is a cordial disagreement, allow them to resolve it without intervention.
- Be available as a good listener. Ask questions that help clarify the problem. Don't take sides, and be sure to apply the people skills you've acquired.
- If the disagreement is hostile, intervene and discuss ways to deal with the issue constructively. Facilitate by asking the parties to state their ideas and ask them to paraphrase each other's perspectives. You may need to require a cooling-down period, after which they meet again (possibly with you) to resolve the problem.

Gloria and Elizabeth were managers who didn't work well together. They didn't like each other, either. They constantly bickered about work goals and procedures. Nearly every week they would individually go to their boss, Dennis, to complain about each other. Dennis listened and encouraged them to focus on the business problems and try to work together as teammates, but as the months went on, there was no improvement. When their issues bubbled over in a staff meeting, Dennis brought the two women together for a separate meeting. He reprimanded them for allowing their differences to disrupt the staff meeting. He reiterated his expectations for allowing staff members to do things differently within set guidelines. He also restated the department values of teamwork and handling conflict constructively.

Dennis asked both managers to state their issues. He listened empathetically to their concerns and positions. Together, they identified ways to deal with each other effectively, and Dennis asked them to commit to working on their business relationship. They agreed. While they didn't always agree with each other, they addressed their issues and worked together in the best interests of their department and customers, and problems were minimized.

Two Methods for Managing Conflict

The primary goal of conflict management is to create a positive and productive working environment. There are two main methodologies for managing conflict that do not squelch performance or break trust:

- The LEAD model
- Constructive confrontation

The LEAD Model

The goal is a win/win resolution to the problem. An excellent supervisor starts with being a good listener, paraphrasing concerns, asking probing questions to gain a clearer understanding, attending to the emotional state of the person(s) with the problem, and finally defining a game plan or solution. You might have to work through this process multiple times before obtaining a workable solution to the problem.

L isten

E xplore.

A ttend.

D efine a solution.

A leader actually seeks out concerns by checking in with employees at regular intervals through proactive one-on-one sessions or daily communication. This requires time and a commitment to people. One supervisor said, "I don't have time to be with my people." Quite frankly, in this fast-paced world, that person doesn't have time to be a leader then!

Addressing concerns means uncovering employee reactions as you discuss needs and issues, clarifying misunderstandings about the problem or the employee's situation, defusing emotions in "sticky" areas, resolving differences that may arise, handling different perspectives, and maintaining open dialogue.

Listen: Your goal is to focus on the employee's needs and objectives, not on your need for a quick resolution to the issue. Ask yourself these things as you prepare to listen:

1. Do you want to listen?
2. Do you make appropriate eye contact?
3. Do you use verbal cues?
   ("Yes," "I see," "Okay")
4. Do you use nonverbal cues?
   (Take notes, nod your head, use positive body language)
5. Do you paraphrase or summarize your understanding of the issue?
   ("What I hear you saying is…." "If I understand you correctly, you mean….")

Explore: Do you know and understand what the other person is trying to say? Use questions to better gain perspective from that person's point of view.

1. Do you maintain your composure and stay professional?
2. Do you use open-ended questions to gain more information?
   (What? How? Where? Why?)
3. Do you use close-ended questions to gain agreement or closure?
   (Yes or no.)
4. Do you use directives to gain additional information?
   ("Tell me more about…." "Explain that again…." "Talk more about….")
5. Do you paraphrase again for understanding?

Attend: Are your attitude and your behavior communicating that you care? Positive communication is a product of three areas: words, tone of voice, and body language. As we mentioned earlier, body language has actually been shown to be the most important of these. What you say is not as important as how you say it!

1. Do you maintain your focus on the person by holding onto your response until you have gained understanding?
2. Do you pay attention to the employee's demeanor and emotions?
3. Do you ask more clarifying questions, if needed?

> "*The leader follows in front.*"
>
> **–Proverb**

Define a solution: Ideally, you'll be approaching a customized solution that is centered on the person or persons you are dealing with. In other words, you are ready to answer based on an understanding of their perspective of the situation or problem.

1. Do you summarize your understanding?
2. Do you specifically respond?
3. Do you close for agreement on the issue, or next steps?

The LEAD model provides balance between understanding, collaborating, and directing behaviors. It decreases resistance in the other person. It allows others and you to "unpack" emotional responses in a constructive manner. Finally, it ensures a focused response that is more likely to address the person's true concerns, and it includes him or her in a problem-solving process. The LEAD model works well because the focus is other-centered, which is a foundation of effective human relations and leadership.

Sometimes the LEAD model doesn't work. No technique is foolproof. People can be unpredictable, and things don't always work out smoothly. At that point, a little constructive confrontation can be useful.

Constructive Confrontation

Use this approach if the conflict becomes more difficult, if those involved are unwilling to follow through on previous agreements, or if the person becomes even more unapproachable. This is a straightforward, direct, yet respectful process. This method requires a step-by-step approach, using language such as the example that follows:

- "[Person's name __________], we have a problem we need to talk about." Use a collective "we" so the person listens without getting defensive.
- "When you [state the issue __________], ..."
- "...I feel [state how you feel in non-judgmental language __________]."
- "I would prefer [tell them how you want them to act __________]."
- "If you [act as requested], then [state a positive outcome __________]." Pause to wait for a response. Most of the most the time the person will become conciliatory and cooperative. If not, take the next step.
- If the person isn't cooperative, restate what you want—the positive outcome)—and then state a consequence for not taking the actions you want.

Here is an example. "Bill, we have a problem we need to talk about. When you don't follow through with the budget numbers we need for our project, I am disappointed by your lack of support for the team. I would prefer you get me the numbers on time as we have discussed. If you do, the entire team will be grateful and on track for reaching our goals. [Pause.] If you don't, I will need to assign you another task and note this matter in your personnel file."

It's been said that the only people without problems are six feet under. Conflict is natural. If you deal with it constructively, you will have more effective communication with your team, and it will unleash their creative juices to solve problems. Without effective conflict management, you will be hard-pressed to build a high-performance team.

> ***"The greater the difficulty, the greater the glory."***
>
> **–Cicero**

CASE STUDY: Best Supervisors!

Pete works for a large international computer manufacturer. He's a customer service supervisor. He has been with the company most of his career and worked his way to his present position.

Pete is a no-nonsense type of manager, but his people like him. He is technically competent and hardworking. Everyone else works hard, too, and Pete allows time off without hesitation for family issues. Each year, Pete attends training programs put on by the company and makes sure his reps do also. He also does monthly service coaching meetings. He has goals and plans that are tracked weekly for results. Each employee knows where he or she stands.

If an employee fails to meet goals, Pete adds a detailed action plan during a coaching session. He uses other options, too, like mentoring and training. If performance doesn't improve over time, the action plan includes a 90-day agreement with consequences, up to and including termination. The plan works 100% of the time. While he has lost a few employees, only one has had to be terminated in 20+ years. Others improve, are transferred to a new job, or find a new company to work for. All of this is done in an open, constructive manner.

What are the strategies that Pete uses?

____

____

____

What can you learn or relearn from this?

____

____

____

____

Compare your answers to the authors' suggested responses in the Appendix.

Part Summary

We have discussed different methods of addressing, handling, and resolving performance problems with employees and conflicts in the workplace. You have also discovered the things that you may already do and some things you need to start working on while dealing with employee problems. We've also discussed the importance of conflict and ways to deal with it openly and constructively.

P A R T **4**

Supervise with Flexibility

"You cannot push anyone up the ladder unless he is willing to climb himself."

–Andrew Carnegie

In this part:

- Situational Supervising

Situational Supervising

Even though you want to be fair and consistent as a supervisor or manager, you can't manage everyone the same way. People are different, and you have to manage them in different ways. How you manage someone depends on the employee and the situation, not on you! Two key questions are:

- ▶ **Will** — Does the employee want to do the job?
- ▶ **Skill** — Can the employee do the job?

Your leadership style shouldn't depend on your personality as much as it depends on the needs of the employee. Ken Blanchard emphasizes the phrase "Different strokes for different folks." Management theorists Blanchard, Hershey, and Goleman have taught the concept of situational leadership for years. Our approach here is to provide a practical and hands-on look at how to vary your approach today with any given employee. Excellent supervisors learn to use a variety of styles, depending on the skill and motivation of the employee. Why do this? So you can accelerate the performance and success of the employee.

A supervisor has to have a well-rounded skill set to handle employees in many different scenarios. For example, if you were a controller, wouldn't you manage an inexperienced accountant differently than a veteran of ten years? Yes! It makes sense, doesn't it? How you supervise long-time employees who take on a new task should be different from how you supervised them in the original job, right? You need a handle the situation differently now that the performance has changed. Successful supervisors ask this question:

> What does the employee need from me to be successful?

The answers echo the questions at the top of this section:

- ▶ **Skill** — For their skills, they need training, teaching, mentoring, and coaching.
- ▶ **Will** — For their motivation, they need communication, support, recognition, and coaching.

In addition, not all things are equal in a person's performance. You need flexibility from one job task to another. For example, a customer service rep may be great at handling complaints and not so good at selling. A different strategy is needed to help this person in each area. Understanding this can give you the keys to motivating employees on a case-by-case basis. By combining skill and will, you get four possibilities for increasing flexibility.

Employee Types and Supervisory Styles

Employees can be classified into four basic types: trainee, learner, dependable, and star. There is a supervisory style that typically works well for with each respective type: instructor, counselor, communicator, and resource. Of course, you will find that most people, and your styles, are a mix of these categories. Following is a table of general types and styles, followed by a more detailed explanation.

An Approach to Flexible Supervision

Dependable Supervisory style: Communicator *High skill*	**Learner** Supervisory style: Counselor *Lower skill*
Star Supervisory style: Resource	**Trainee** Supervisory style: Instructor

Notice in each case there is a supervisory style that best fits the employee.

- **Instructor style** — The primary focus is training; the new employee should be motivated and excited about the new job. New employees who want to learn and work hard are golden. If he or she isn't upbeat about the new job, you made a hiring mistake. Early warnings include being late to work or being absent, having problems with other employees, lacking progress on the job, and taking extra days off because of personal problems. Again, seek your human resources or personnel department's advice, but the best thing to do with employees who have these problems early on is to terminate them before their probation period is up.

- **Counselor style** — After a few months on the job, two things happen: the person learns and makes progress; and the person becomes a little frustrated. The job isn't what he thought it was, or there have been a few mistakes, or his initial enthusiasm has waned a bit. The focus for the leader is to keep training and teaching and paying attention to the emotional impact on the employee's motivation.

- **Communicator style** — Use this style with dependable employees. They have the skills and don't need to be taught, other than for ongoing training for skills development or training in process or product changes. What dependable employees need is a supervisor who can notice a subtle difference in the efforts that affect their productivity. This is where an excellent supervisor shines—a little communication, recognition, and support can go a long way.

- **Resource style** — Use this style with a star employee. Stars are usually your best performers, and they have the skills and the will to do well. Except for ongoing training and education, you don't have to teach them the job or motivate them. They are self-motivated. Your goal is to encourage them, bounce ideas off of them, and delegate assignments to them.

Style Flexibility Summary

- Trainee = Instructor style
  - Lower skill, higher will regarding the new job or task
  - Needs specific training and direction
- Learner = Counselor style
  - Some skill, varied will; will declines after initial experience
  - Needs specific training in some areas; also needs to be motivated
- Dependable employee = Communicator style
  - Higher skill, varied will; some days the person is "on," and some days she is not
  - Needs support and help when not motivated; usually doesn't need specific job-task help. You can delegate to this person on occasion.
- Star = Resource style
  - Highest skill, highest will
  - Needs a resource to kick around ideas with; can do the job alone; stay out of his way. You can delegate to this person more.

Style flexibility is an intricate skill that can make a big difference. Remember this axiom: small things done consistently in strategic places have major impact. So, adjust as needed to better help each individual employee.

> ***"To improve your team's performance, you have to improve your performance first."***
>
> **–Rick Conlow**

Performance Management Reminder

All employees need the following no matter what their will or skill levels:

1. **Clear goals and expectations**
2. **Recognition and praise for a job well done**
3. **Help with problems**
4. **Coaching for development**

The Chronic Poor Performer

What we have discussed so far is designed to eliminate problems and improve performance. But sometimes, things don't improve. There is a potential fifth group of employees sometimes referred to as "deadwood." An employee in this category consistently is a low performer and a chronic problem. What do you do with an employee in this group? If redirection, coaching, and confrontation fail, then fire him. But before you terminate someone, make sure you've done all you can to help. Set goals, train, give recognition, coach, and be a good communicator.

Managers are often too slow to fire. Remember the mini/max principle: the minimum performance you allow becomes the maximum you can expect. By following the goal setting process outlined earlier, you'll be better able to detect and deal with low performance.

Follow your company's policy when you have to fire someone. Generally, most procedures include:

- One or two oral warnings
- One or two written warnings
- Suspension
- Termination

When going through a process like this, always focus on specific job-performance issues, and not on generalities like attitude. Remember to keep documentation to track your efforts to help an employee. Be factual, not judgmental. Firing can be a very delicate process. It affects the livelihood of the employee and it is costly for a company. Do what's right and seek advice from your manager and your company's legal or human resources departments.

Some Supervisory Style Tips

Instructor	**Counselor**
Give specific directions and OJT	Focus on talks and motivation
Train and demonstrate	Explain specifics
Train more; take the time	Train and demonstrate where needed
Set goals for the employee	Give helpful suggestions
Supervise closely	Set goals with some involvement
Praise progress	Give regular positive feedback
Redirect on problems	Redirect or review problems
Communicator	**Resource**
Listen and ask questions	Don't get in the way
Focus on motivation	Be available if necessary
Delegate sometimes	Ask about goals
Be readily available	Give recognition for results
Review progress periodically	Challenge the person with delegated tasks or opportunities
Discuss goals together	Ask for ideas; delegate
Handle problems quickly	Review or reprimand when problems occur
Review or reprimand when problems occur	

SUPERVISING WITH STYLE FLEXIBILITY

Determine the employee type and the supervisory style in the scenarios below.

1. An experienced technician was given an urgent job by his supervisor to fix a comeback and is complaining about the lead time. He is highly skilled and has the competence to do the job effectively. In the past, he has always completed jobs well and on time.

   Employee type: ______________________________

   Supervisory style: ______________________________

2. You asked one of your experienced employees to train a new cashier. The training didn't get done properly, and delays in paperwork have resulted, which are making customers irritable. This is the third time this year something like this has happened with this person.

   Employee type: ______________________________

   Supervisory style: ______________________________

3. An employee asked if she could take an extra day off around the Thanksgiving holiday. This person has developed a good rapport with all and, overall, has significantly helped deliver excellent service.

   Employee type: ______________________________

   Supervisory style: ______________________________

4. One of your reliable, longer-term employees has been on a new job assignment the last few months as a lead person in the service department. Lately, as you have pushed to meet the numbers, problems have increased. You have received complaints from customers about her.

   Employee type: ______________________________

   Supervisory style: ______________________________

5. One of your veteran bookkeepers is accurate and very skilled in accounting. However, some customers think he is rude. You have talked to him about this twice before.

   Employee type: ______________________________

   Supervisory style: ______________________________

CONTINUED

P A R T 5

Lead a High-Energy Work Environment

"Positive feedback increases the sense of competence, while negative feedback undermines it."

–Edward L. Deci

In this part:

- Praise, Recognition, and Celebration
- Energizing Your Team

Praise, Recognition, and Celebration

What motivates people? If you recall our earlier discussions, recognition is a prime motivator. This is the positive side of giving feedback. People want to be noticed and valued for what they do. According to research, 91% of employees want more recognition at work, and only half say they get any at all. Gallup's research found that employees who said they were recognized in the last week tended to perform better than those who don't get recognized as often. Contrast this with the fact that most supervisors or managers don't realize that praised behavior will be repeated, and most think it is wrong to brag about an employee in front of others.

A supervisor reported that after giving recognition to an employee, the employee cried. When asked why, she said, "I have worked here for 26 years and you are the first person to give me recognition for my job." While this may be an extreme case, it points out a common weakness in the leadership style of many.

Some Key Principles for Recognition

There are several key principles to follow when giving recognition.

- **Be genuine** — Give recognition from the heart because an employee earned and deserves it based on progress or exemplary performance. Give the recognition also because you care about and value your employees.
- **Be specific** — For example, "Josh, you did a great job solving that quality problem and identifying an action plan for improvement. You are a true team player and I am delighted with the results." Do this as opposed to simply saying, "Great job!" or "Super!" or "Way to go." Your people won't know what you mean; they can see through phoniness.
- **Be personable** — Think in terms individual needs. Different people prefer a variety of approaches. Be verbal and private with some, and verbal and public with others. If you can give rewards, for example, provide a gift certificate to a sporting goods store to one employee and to a restaurant for another.
- **Be immediate** — Give recognition as quickly as possible. The longer you wait, the less effective it is. Saying "thank you" today to someone who did an on-the-job training assignment for you six months ago is too late and counterproductive. Do it now. Saying "thank you" at the time the work is done is much more powerful.
- **Be public** — Consider the employee when you do this. Usually public recognition is good because others see it and this helps reinforce the behaviors of high performance. Use e-mail, company newsletters, or bulletin boards for this.

- **Stay positive** — Recognize people's performance for quality, productivity, sales, customer service, or timeliness. Do it constructively, following these overall guidelines. Don't throw in criticism with it on something people need to do better.
- **Recognize often** — You don't have to praise every little thing employees do; you do need to genuinely appreciate their efforts. They will respond with increased performance, and they will choose to go the extra mile. Too often, supervisors get busy, forget to recognize employees, and forget (or don't know) the motivational value that recognition can provide. Pay attention and notice the efforts that people are putting into their jobs. Look for ways to compliment people on their efforts daily. Research suggests that we need to praise each employee in some way at least weekly.
- **Be persistent** — Genuine recognition of employees will create a wholesome work atmosphere, but it requires persistence and creativity. Stick with it and try different things. Remember that you are recognizing employees because it matters. You are positively affecting someone's life, not merely motivating for performance. With consistent recognition, you fan the flames of a person's internal motivation and desire to excel. You also build the person's confidence and his or her loyalty to you and your company.

A certain Canadian company consistently performs better than the competition in service, sales, and profits. When you walk into this company's offices, you sense a difference. Throughout the location, you see employee recognition: employee pictures on the walls, goals listed on white boards and bulletin boards, and charts and graphs posted to show progress. Also, plaques, trophies, and certificates for achievements adorn the meeting rooms. Contrast that environment with a business in Minneapolis that posted an employee-of-the-month picture in the entryway of the offices. The last posted award was December, and the current month was July. Video cameras also taped employee work areas. Needless to say, employee morale was low in the company.

Which place would you rather work? Which place would bring out the best in you? Supervisors who do not give positive recognition and praise typically have two big excuses: 1) they don't have time for it, and 2) they hire good people who "know what to do and don't need a babysitter." This is dinosaur thinking. Excellent supervisors find the time for employee recognition; poor ones don't. Employee recognition can be built into the fabric of your daily communication and leadership practices without taking extra time. Consistent recognition will help you create rock-solid relationships with people, build their pride in their work, and achieve your goals more readily.

Informal and Formal Recognition

It's natural for the human spirit to desire praise, recognition, and appreciation. During an Excellence in Management workshop, we reviewed the concept of effective recognition and then gave the managers in attendance a "live action" assignment to go recognize two of their employees. At first, the supervisors and managers resisted the idea because their employees weren't at the workshop. We listened to their concerns and brainstormed alternatives to face-to-face conversations: phone, fax, or e-mail. Each person had to complete a form that stated whom they called, described how they gave recognition, and described the reaction of the employee. We even promised recognition-dessert of their choice at lunch if they completed the assignment! At lunchtime, the heartwarming stories of surprise and appreciation of employees rolled in. The power of simple recognition was amazing.

Informal Recognition

Unfortunately, giving informal recognition seemed to be a challenge for many of the managers. We chuckle in recollection of a supervisor who needed extra coaching because he didn't quite get the concept. When we asked how the call to his employee went, he responded, "Okay; I asked them, 'what great thing did you do for me today that I should recognize?'" He obviously still needed help with the concept.

Informal recognition is a key ingredient to healthy relationships with employees. Regular and consistent informal recognition makes employees feel appreciated, respected, and valued. It involves praising them for progress on a goal, project, or other successful endeavor.

Informal recognition…

- is for everyday activities done well,
- costs little or nothing,
- focuses on specific behavior, progress, or results,
- strengthens the person-to-person relationship, and
- has an immediate positive impact.

For example: "Good job, Bill! Thanks for taking the time to help that customer. You were already busy but took the time anyway. Your efforts made me excited about our commitment to customer service."

It takes a few seconds to give praise like this. But in order to do this, you have to be engaged, observing, and working with employees at various times. How else will you see or hear what's going on? Informal recognition is not about looking over people's shoulders and saying "Good job!" for everything they do. Informal recognition is an ongoing process of praising and rewarding good behavior, thereby communicating that people are valued on your team. It needs to be a genuine and regular practice to be effective.

Imagine the impact on employees if this became part of your regular supervisory practices. How would employees feel? What kind of job would they do? Behavioral scientists say that praised behavior will be repeated. Good bosses learn to master informal recognition so that it is a seamless part of their day-to-day communication. Their employees and co-workers want to come to work; they do a good job because they feel good about it. Bad bosses struggle with recognition in any form and are forever critical. Employees avoid those bosses and can't wait to go home at the end of the day.

"And put up a big, splashy banner that says, 'Thank you, Peasants'."

TOP 10 INFORMAL METHODS OF RECOGNITION

Check any methods that you have used. Add one or two from your own experience.

____ 1. Verbal praise, privately

____ 2. Verbal praise in a group

____ 3. Appreciative e-mail message

____ 4. Verbal praise plus a cup of coffee, water, or soda

____ 5. An e-mail message with creative graphics to say thank you

____ 6. Thank-you note with a personal message

____ 7. Thank-you card

____ 8. Letter of commendation

____ 9. Token of appreciation (candy, card, sticker, or balloon) with a positive message

____ 10. Buying the employee lunch

11. Others:

____ ____

____ ____

What do you do well?

____

____

What can you do more of?

____

____

Formal Recognition

Many supervisors or managers don't use formal recognition programs because they have limited or no budgets. Public organizations often use that excuse, but it is still possible to give recognition—it just takes more ingenuity on a limited budget. Robert Nelson's book *1001 Ways to Recognize Employees* provides numerous specific and creative ways to reward people.

Formal recognition…

- focuses on achieving goals,
- can cost money,
- requires specific criteria or performance indicators,
- spans specific timeframes (week, month, quarter, or year), and
- emphasizes top performance.

For example: "It's my pleasure, Sue, to award you this STAR plaque for outstanding customer service last month according to our surveys! Thank you for your incredible contributions."

Formal recognition needs to focus on the primary goals of the department or team. Without clear goals, it is difficult to do formal recognition. With clear goals and performance standards, you can praise your team to success.

Read the following sample memo.

To: All Employees

Subject: A special Thank You

Last week's record-breaking cold weather brought out the "true grit" in all of us. It was gratifying to see so many employees helping customers and fellow employees with many problems resulting from the cold weather.

On Monday morning, my desk was filled with employee "Good Deed" cards expressing appreciation for helping each other by fixing heaters, starting cars, plowing snow, giving rides, and working late to get customers' cars on the road.

Thanks for your pride in customer and employee satisfaction!

Dave

All of Dave's employees received a copy of this note, and Dave personally talked to many of them. Dave retired after a long career as an executive in a large automobile dealer organization. It is plain to see why his business was a leader in customer and employee loyalty. While this could be an example of informal recognition, we show it in this section on formal recognition because it exemplifies the high-performance culture that good bosses nurture.

Rick owns a tire franchise. During the first part of his career, he ran stores for the corporation. Every store he managed, excelled and was among the most profitable stores in the company. Rick was put in a number of losing stores and turned them around in a year. The company wanted to promote him to the head office, but he didn't want to relocate, nor did he want to travel, which would take him away from his family, so he bought a franchise. Within a year of buying the store, he was called to active duty for Operation Desert Storm. While most small businesses would die with their owner gone for six months, his thrived. He set up a support network of professionals to help in his absence, but more than that, his employees stepped up to the plate. Rick had invested in them so that when he needed their help the most, they came through.

The following are some of Rick's excellent supervisory practices:

- Buy a birthday cake and have a celebration for each new employee.
- Hold regular cookouts to celebrate employee successes.
- Conduct goal-setting sessions for both job-related and personal goals.
- Hold ongoing meetings to focus on and recognize superior customer service.
- Help with financial problems or down payments on a house.
- Treat all employees as professionals and seek their input on issues.
- Give bonuses for higher productivity.

When Rick first opened the store, he asked his team of 20 employees how they wanted to be treated—as professionals or as hired hands? He told them that pros come to work and do whatever it takes to care for customers on any given day, and they share in the profits. Hired hands punch in and punch out, get an hourly wage, and work by the clock. His employees unanimously agreed to be treated as professionals. Most brought their families in to tour the new business.

Methods such as these reinforce and bring out the inherent pride people feel when they do well, achieve goals, and are part of something worthwhile. Let's review formal recognition.

TOP 10 WAYS TO GIVE FORMAL RECOGNITION

Check any of the methods that you have used. Add one or two from your own experience.

____ 1. Certificates of recognition

____ 2. Incentives or bonuses

____ 3. Plaques or trophies

____ 4. Electronic gadgets

____ 5. Gift certificates

____ 6. Name in the company newsletter or publication

____ 7. Lunch or dinner

____ 8. Time off

____ 9. Award banquets

____ 10. Trips

11. Others:

____ ____

____ ____

What do you do well?

____

____

____

What can you do more of?

____

____

____

The Greatest Leadership Technique of All Time

In a nutshell, the greatest supervisory technique of all time is this: what gets reviewed, reinforced, and recognized gets done! Reinforce, recognize, and reward the behavior you want and need, and you will achieve outstanding results!

Now What?

Go recognize your employees! Seek out the things they do right and tell them, regularly. John Wooden, former coach of the UCLA Bruins, won 10 NCAA championships in 12 years. It's been said that John Wooden was 99% positive with his team. When he saw a mistake, he showed the player the right way to do the job, not the wrong way. He did this over and over. Besides fostering teamwork, this positive reinforcement approach greatly aided his success on the basketball court. It will also help you achieve supervisory excellence.

Energizing Your Team

The number-one reason people go to work is because they have to! Their alarm goes off every morning and they get up reluctantly to trudge off to work. Some people put in eight, ten, twelve hours a day, year after year, and find no enjoyment in their work. One research study says 77% of people are looking for a different job. If that's what is going on and people want to leave, how effective are they in their jobs? Why does it have to be that way?

Sam was the VP of training for a large U.S. retailer. For eight years, he traveled from his home on one end of the country to the corporate headquarters on the other end. He did a great job creating a high-performance and enjoyable corporate culture. He developed training programs, incentive initiatives, and employee recognition programs for customer service and internal teamwork. He earned the nickname "Doctor of Fun." He always had a smile, a hearty laugh, a kind word for others, and a sense of humor. Unfortunately, many of the other executives didn't get it. They cared more about Wall Street's analysis, store sales, and profits—and that's what they focused on. The worse the numbers were, the more they pushed and yelled and added metrics and action steps, none of which worked. They didn't understand the High Performance formula and the elegance of consistently creating a climate that was ripe with recognition, training, coaching, excitement, and fun! After a period of time, Sam was asked to retire because he didn't fit their corporate mantra.

How do you energize the workplace? Start with an open mind. While a company needs to make money, most companies can afford to lighten up a bit. (Thank goodness for "casual day" on Friday.)

Fire Up the Workplace

Everything this book has discussed thus far will contribute to a more enjoyable work environment. Clear expectations, fair treatment, problem solving, recognition, and effective communication will all help employees like their jobs more and perform better. The following three activities can "fire up" the workplace, put some electricity in the air, and create a work atmosphere that is fun, productive, and rewarding.

- Team activities
- Social activities
- Communication activities

Team Activities

With this strategy, you divide your work area into smaller teams to get the job done or special activities completed. All companies have projects that need completion and business segments that need improvement. Teams can be an effective means to get things accomplished. Teams bring out the best in employees—more ideas, stronger commitment, greater involvement, and much more fun. If you get everyone on a team, they can work together on a wide range of process improvement business activities, in areas such as:

- Accounts receivable
- Sales results
- Customer service results
- Product delivery or quality
- Safety

The list could go on, and the possibilities are great, but beware lest team processes become boring, burdensome, or overloaded with an endless litany of metrics and procedural reviews. These very things have bogged down some high-quality business management initiatives. To avoid the drain and maintain some fun, lighten up the team effort. Here are seven actions we have found to help energize a team:

1. Name your teams.
2. Create a logo for every team.
3. Create a banner for every team (see the example).
4. Get polo shirts, T-shirts, or caps embroidered with team names.
5. Design a colorful goal board for tracking results.
6. Train employees on how to participate on an effective team.
7. Award team participation or milestone accomplishments with fantastic prizes.

The Sea Captains

We CREATE the "Perfect Storm"

Persistent | **Confident** | **Stable in Rough Seas**

Calvin is the service manager for a company in Victoria, British Columbia. We worked with him and his company. As a result, he divided his customer service reps into two teams: the Guns and the Roses. They had polo shirts and caps made for each team. Throughout the year, they tracked the service and sales results of the teams. In their weekly meetings, they recognized team results and gave team awards. They did team competitions, team cheers, and team training. The reps had a lot of fun, worked hard, achieved excellent results, and built lasting camaraderie.

Communication Activities

Good communication, aimed at increasing the energy of employees, is similar to having an internal marketing plan. Just as you attract customers with effective marketing, you also need to have a plan for getting and keeping your employees' attention. Try the following as a benchmark for best practices.

Top 10 Communication Activities for Your Team

Check the methods that you have used. Add one or two from your own experience.

____ 1. Decorate your work area or lunchroom.

____ 2. Use bulletin boards to post positive messages.

____ 3. Hang banners, balloons, and other props that relate to your goals.

____ 4. Have a Wall of Fame with employees' pictures and their accomplishments and successes.

____ 5. Send weekly team e-mail messages with some color or pizzazz to encourage and inspire employees to work toward the goals.

____ 6. Send weekly individual e-mail or text messages to individuals.

____ 7. Set up a bulletin board or intranet dashboard to track results.

____ 8. Use an internal newsletter for recognition, info on plans, updates on progress, and humor.

____ 9. Hold short team "power" meetings daily or weekly to discuss progress.

____ 10. Hold weekly or monthly one-on-one coaching sessions with members of your team.

11. Others:

____ ____

____ ____

Social Activities

Everyone loves a party, and while we don't suggest partying all the time, there are companies that never loosen up! Americans work more hours than employees in any other developed country around the world. Yet, nearly three-fourths of workers today say they would quit their jobs if they could. The truth is that uptight and bored employees don't do the best work. They are just showing up for that paycheck.

Recently, a flight attendant for a major U.S. airline said, "I hate people. They are just like cattle. All I want to do is serve them quickly and get away from them and read my book." Whoa! Maybe that was just one worker's opinion, but while at a hotel in a major U.S. city, we watched the same airline's graduation exercises for a new class of flight attendants in an adjoining meeting room. During a break, we went over and told one of their leaders, "This is nice to see." His matter-of-fact reply was, "No, you don't understand; this is 40 more votes for the union." That airline had serious morale and service issues, and it had recently gone through bankruptcy.

Can't people be excited and do a great job, too? Professional athletes play their childhood games for a living; they excel and seem to hold onto the fun. Since we spend a good portion of our lives on the job, we need to make it more enjoyable while achieving the corporate objectives. To have employee loyalty, you have to earn it.

> ***"The art of good management is making difficult things simple, not simple things difficult."***
>
> **–Anonymous**

We helped one company improve its customer service scores to all-time high levels in four months. The company had been working at it for four years with little progress. Why did it finally improve? We set clear expectations and goals, communicated regularly about progress, provided new tools through training and social activities, and provided lots of recognition. You can do this, too!

A Final Thought To Ponder

You end up with mediocre performance, at best, if you and your employees do the "same old, same old" every day. To tap into tremendous employee potential, use some of the strategies we have discussed. Keep in mind the principles we reviewed on what motivates people. If you can get the job done better and have some sense of excitement and fun, it would make a difference, right?

Certainly you have to do the job and do it well. Not everything is fun or high powered. But why not jazz it up a bit? This one thing we know, a team with energy is much better than a team with lethargy.

Top 10 Social Activities for Your Team

Check the methods that you have used. Add one or two from your own experience.

____ 1. After-work sports teams: softball, hockey, etc.

____ 2. Going to professional baseball or football games, etc.

____ 3. After-work pizza parties

____ 4. Surprise birthday parties

____ 5. Golf tournaments

____ 6. Comedy club or theatre dinner evenings

____ 7. Zoo or museum days

____ 8. Team lunch meetings

____ 9. Business retreats

____ 10. Holiday parties

11. Others:

____ ____

____ ____

What do you do well?

____

____

____

What can you do more of?

____

____

____

Part Summary

We have discussed different methods of motivating and recognizing employees and getting their attention. You are now able to use these methods and create your own teamwork activities to entice employees to perform even better at work. With this information, you can use a variety of approaches in the right situations to create a high-performance work environment.

A P P E N D I X

Appendix to Part 1

Comments & Suggested Responses

Case Study: An Excellent Supervisor

Answers may vary, but they could mention that Shirley used the following strategies:

- She set monthly productivity goals and plans with her associates.
- She divided her employees into seven teams and held a meeting with each team to begin the process.
- She had each team create a name for themselves and make charts to track progress.
- They agreed that if they hit the goal, she would buy lunch.
- She rewarded their efforts.

Appendix to Part 3

Comments & Suggested Responses

Case Study: Best Supervisors!

Answers may vary, but could mention that Pete uses the following strategies:

- He attends training programs and makes sure his reps do, too.
- He holds monthly service coaching meetings.
- He has goals and plans that are tracked weekly for results.
- If an employee fails to meet goals, Pete adds a detailed action plan during a coaching session.
- The action plan includes a 90-day agreement with consequences, up to and including termination.
- He mentors and trains as needed.

Appendix to Part 4

Comments & Suggested Responses

Supervising with Style Flexibility

Here are suggested answers and the reasons for them. If your answers differ, explain why.

1. Dependable/Communicator

   He's an experienced employee, and even though he complained a bit, there isn't a performance problem.

2. Dependable/Coach

   This is an experienced employee who performed poorly as a trainer. Does the person know how to train? Was enough time made available? You need to coach this person, give him the opportunity to learn the needed skills, and provide the time needed to train the new cashier. You might need to reprimand if you've already done the coaching appropriately.

3. Star/Resource

   This employee has developed excellent performance and is good with others. If you can free up the time, why not give the extra day off if the lead time is appropriate?

4. Learner/Instructor

   This person has been a lead for a few months. She has the required technical skill but needs training (classroom, OJT) to learn the people skills this position requires.

5. Dependable/Coach

   This is a veteran employee who has good technical skills. He needs coaching to deal with his poor performance with customers.

6. Star/Resource

   The employee consistently performs well and seems to try new things to improve.

7. Deadwood

   Over six months, the performance is getting worse, even though you have talked to him several times. Chances are, you need to terminate this employee.

8. Trainee/Instructor and Star/Resource

   We have two goals here: product knowledge and customer service. Continue working with this person to learn more about the products. Give this person some praise for progress. This person has great results on customer service, so be sure to give positive feedback for that.

9. Learner/Instructor

   This employee is still learning and needs ongoing training from you or others.

10. Dependable/Communicator

    Job results are good and consistent, not exceptional. Yet there are signs of a potential problem. You may want to have an informal talk with him.

Viva-Crisp 50-Minute
Titles in the Series

ISBN	Author	Title	YOP	Price
9788130918174	Gambino	**50 Minutes to Better Software Demos**: *Apply Your Sales Skills with Confidence*	2011	195.00
9788130918488	Bozek	**50 One-Minute Tips to Better Communications**: *Speak, Write and Present More Effectively, 3/e*	2011	250.00
9788130918211	Conlow & Watsabaugh	**Achieving Supervisory Excellence**: *Be the Leader Your People Need*	2011	195.00
9788130918396	McKnight & Chapman	**Attitude**: *Protect Your Most Priceless Asset, 5/e*	2011	245.00
9788130918495	Terry Dickey	**Basics of Budgeting**: *Become a Better Business Planner, 2/e*	2011	250.00
9788130918310	Conlow & Watsabaugh	**Become a Successful Supervisor**: *Develop Essential People Skills*	2011	225.00
9788130918327	Brock	**Better Business Writing**: *Become A More Powerful Communicator, 5/e*	2011	225.00
9788130918228	Dupont	**Business Etiquette & Professionalism**: *Conduct Yourself With Confidence, 3/e*	2011	195.00
9788130918181	Morgan	**Calming Upset Customers**: *Stay in Control ... In any Situation, 4/e*	2011	195.00
9788130918198	Minor	**Coaching and Counseling**: *Become a Better Manager Through Mentoring, 4/e*	2011	195.00
9788130918273	Decker	**Communication Skills for Leaders**: *Deliver a Clear and Consistent Message, 4/e*	2011	225.00
9788130918143	Kindler	**Conflict Management**: *Resolve Disagreement at Work, 4/e*	2011	165.00
9788130918280	Conlow & Watsabaugh	**Creating a High Performance Team**: *Gain the Skills of Today's Successful Leaders*	2011	225.00
9788130918334	Feldman	**Critical Thinking**: *Make Strategic Decisions With Confidence, 2/e*	2011	225.00
9788130918426	Flynn	**E-Mail Management**: *Keep Your Inbox Under Control, 2/e*	2011	245.00
9788130918471	Kravitz & Schubert	**Emotional Intelligence Works**: *Think, Be and Work Smarter, 3/e*	2011	245.00
9788130918150	Maddux	**Ethics in Business**: *Manage With Authority and Fairness, 2/e*	2011	195.00
9788130918235	Rouillard	**Goals and Goal Setting**: *Achieve Measurable Results, 4/e*	2011	195.00
9788130918204	Conlow Watsabaugh	**Handling Difficult People and Situations**: *Lead People Through Adversity*	2011	195.00

ISBN	Author	Title	YOP	Price
9788130918433	Wendover	**High Performance Hiring**: *Select the Best Every Time, 3/e*	2011	245.00
9788130918402	Shea	**Making the Most of Being Mentored**: *Mentors Help Mentees Do, 2/e*	2011	245.00
9788130918242	Scott	**Managing Personal Change**: *Stay Positive and Stay in Control*, 3/e	2011	195.00
9788130918341	Haynes	**Meeting Skills for Leaders**: *Make Meetings More Productive, 4/e*	2011	225.00
9788130918440	Shea	**Mentoring**: *Make It A Mutually Rewarding Experience, 4/e*	2011	245.00
9788130918525	Shandler	**Motivating the Millennial Knowledge Worker**: *Help Today's Workforce Succeed in Today's Economy*	2011	395.00
9788130918167	Mandel	**Presentation Skills**: *Captivate and Educate Your Audience, 4/e*	2011	195.00
9788130918518	Pokras	**Problem Solving for Teams**: *Make Consensus More Achievable, 3/e*	2011	295.00
9788130918259	Haynes	**Project Management**: *Get from the Idea to Implementation Successfully, 4/e*	2011	195.00
9788130918372	Martin	**Quality Customer Service**: *Satisfy Customers–It's Everybody's Job, 5/e*	2011	245.00
9788130918457	Lightle & Doucet	**Sexual Harassment in the Workplace**: *Create a Better Workplace For Everyone, 3/e*	2011	245.00
9788130918501	Lengefeld	**Study Skills Strategies**: *Get the Most From Every Minute of Learning, 4/e*	2011	250.00
9788130918358	Conlow & Watsabaugh	**SuperSTAR Customer Service**: *It's all about C.A.R.E.*	2011	225.00
9788130918297	Maddux & Wingfield	**Team Building**: *Turn Personal Strengths Into Group Success, 5/e*	2011	225.00
9788130918464	Finch	**Telephone Courtesy & Customer Service**: *Be Your Company's Lifeline to Customers, 4/e*	2011	245.00
9788130918389	Conlow & Watsabaugh	**Telephone Skills that Satisfy Customers**: *Unleash the Full Potential of the Telephone*	2011	245.00
9788130918303	Romero	**The Business of Listening**: *Become a More Effective Listener, 4/e*	2011	225.00
9788130918365	Chapman & McKnight	**The New Supervisor**: *Lead With Confidence, 5/e*	2011	225.00
9788130918266	Haynes	**Time Management**: *Get An Extra Day a Week*	2011	195.00
9788130918419	Gill & Chatton	**Understanding Financial Statements**: *Master the Tools That Help You Succeed, 3/e*	2011	245.00